EAGLE® BRAND
HOLIDAY
MAGIC IN MINUTES

Publications International, Ltd.

Favorite Brand Name Recipes at www.fbnr.com

Eagle Brand Project Coordinators: Sanford Fink and Joanne Klein

Photography: Peter Dean Ross Photographs
Photographers: Alex Atevich, Peter Dean Ross
Photographers' Assistant: Cynthia Fandl
Prop Stylist: Carey Thornton
Food Stylists: Kim Hartman, Moisette Sintov McNerney
Assistant Food Stylist: Nina Baratto

Pictured on the front cover *(clockwise from top left):* Creamy Hot Chocolate
(page 77), Double Delicious Cookie Bars *(page 42),* Lemon Crumb Bars *(page 46),*
Chocolate Chip Treasure Cookies *(page 32)* and Chocolate Snowswirl Fudge
(page 84).

Pictured on the back cover *(clockwise from top left):* S'Mores on a Stick
(page 26), Mini Cheesecakes *(page 8),* Chocolate Nut Bars *(page 44)* and Sweet
Potato Pecan Pie *(page 52).*

ISBN: 0-7853-7900-2

Manufactured in U.S.A.

8 7 6 5 4 3 2 1

Microwave Cooking: Microwave ovens vary in wattage. Use the cooking times as
guidelines and check for doneness before adding more time.

Preparation/Cooking Times: Preparation times are based on the approximate
amount of time required to assemble the recipe before cooking, baking, chilling or
serving. These times include preparation steps such as measuring, chopping and
mixing. The fact that some preparations and cooking can be done simultaneously
is taken into account. Preparation of optional ingredients and serving suggestions
is not included.

Table of Contents

For more holiday magic visit us at
www.eaglebrand.com

MAKE MAGIC IN MINUTES

For over 144 years,

Eagle Brand has been America's #1 trusted brand of sweetened condensed milk. Since 1856, bakers have been depending on all-natural Eagle® Brand Sweetened Condensed Milk to help them bake all kinds of indulgent desserts and sweet treats. There are three varieties of Eagle Brand: **Original**, *introduced in 1856*; **Low Fat**, *introduced in 1994*; and **Fat Free**, *introduced in 1995*. All three provide the rich, creamy, sweet taste that's the delicious secret to making fabulous desserts, candies, beverages and treats.

THE LITTLE CAN OF MAGIC

Eagle Brand is a unique blend of milk and sugar condensed by a special vacuum process. Since sugar is added during the manufacturing process, most recipes do not require additional sugar. When combined with an acidic ingredient, like lemon juice, sweetened condensed milk thickens without beating to form velvety pie fillings, puddings and other creamy desserts.

THEY'RE DIFFERENT

Evaporated milk and Eagle Brand Sweetened Condensed Milk are two completely different products and are not interchangeable in recipes. As noted earlier, a rich creamy mixture forms when Eagle Brand is combined with acidic juices. On the other hand, when evaporated milk is mixed with acidic juices, the mixture curdles and separates.

INTRODUCTION

KEEP IT IN THE CUPBOARD

Store Eagle Brand in a cool dry place for up to 24 months. Since it is a natural product, the color and consistency may vary from can to can. The product will become thicker and darker in color the longer it is stored, but rest assured it is still good to use.

WINNING THE WAR WITH EAGLE BRAND

Gail Borden introduced Eagle Brand Sweetened Condensed Milk in 1856 to combat food poisoning and other illnesses due to poor preserving techniques and lack of refrigeration. During the Civil War, soldiers turned to Eagle Brand for a milk alternative that wouldn't spoil. It was also used heavily during World War I and World War II. Today the magic of Eagle Brand is synonymous with dreamy desserts and tasty treats.

Now that you know the story behind Eagle Brand, it's time to open a can and let the magic begin!

It Takes the Cake

Mini Cheesecakes

Prep Time: 20 minutes   Bake Time: 20 minutes

1½ cups graham cracker or chocolate wafer crumbs
¼ cup sugar
¼ cup (½ stick) butter or margarine, melted
3 (8-ounce) packages cream cheese, softened
1 (14-ounce) can EAGLE® BRAND Sweetened Condensed
    Milk (NOT evaporated milk)
3 eggs
2 teaspoons vanilla extract

1. Preheat oven to 300°F. Combine graham cracker crumbs, sugar and butter; press equal portions onto bottoms of 24 lightly greased or paper-lined muffin cups.

2. In large mixing bowl, beat cream cheese until fluffy. Gradually beat in **Eagle Brand** until smooth. Add eggs and vanilla; mix well. Spoon equal amounts of mixture (about 3 tablespoons) into prepared cups. Bake 20 minutes or until cakes spring back when lightly touched. Cool.* Chill. Garnish as desired. Refrigerate leftovers.

Makes 2 dozen mini cheesecakes

*If greased muffin cups are used, cool baked cheesecakes. Freeze 15 minutes; remove with narrow spatula. Proceed as above.

Chocolate Mini Cheesecakes: Melt 1 cup (6-ounces) semi-sweet chocolate chips; mix into batter. Proceed as above. Bake 20 to 25 minutes.

Raspberry Swirl Cheesecake

Prep Time: 15 minutes   Bake Time: 25 minutes
Chill Time: 4 hours

**1½ cups fresh or thawed lightly sweetened loose-pack frozen
red raspberries**
**1 (14-ounce) can EAGLE® BRAND Sweetened Condensed
Milk (NOT evaporated milk), divided**
2 (8-ounce) packages cream cheese, softened
3 eggs
2 (6-ounce) chocolate-flavored crumb pie crusts
**Chocolate and white chocolate leaves (recipe follows,
optional)**
Fresh raspberries (optional)

1. Preheat oven to 350°F. In blender container, blend 1½ cups
raspberries until smooth; press through sieve to remove seeds. Stir
⅓ cup **Eagle Brand** into sieved raspberries; set aside.

2. With mixer, beat cream cheese, eggs and remaining **Eagle Brand**
in large bowl. Spoon into crusts. Drizzle with raspberry mixture. With
table knife, gently swirl raspberry mixture through cream cheese
mixture.

3. Bake 25 minutes or until center is nearly set when shaken. Cool;
chill at least 4 hours. Garnish with chocolate leaves and fresh
raspberries, if desired. Store leftovers covered in refrigerator.

Makes 16 servings

Chocolate Leaves: Place 1 (1-ounce) square semi-sweet chocolate
in microwave-safe bowl. Microwave at HIGH (100% power) 1 to
2 minutes, stirring every minute until smooth. With small, clean
paintbrush, paint several coats of melted chocolate on the undersides
of nontoxic leaves, such as mint, lemon or strawberry. Wipe off any
chocolate from top sides of leaves. Place leaves, chocolate sides up,
on waxed-paper-lined baking sheet or on curved surface, such as
rolling pin. Refrigerate leaves until chocolate is firm. To use, carefully
peel leaves away from chocolate.

Creamy Baked Cheesecake

Prep Time: 20 minutes   Bake Time: 55 to 60 minutes
Chill Time: 4 hours

1¼ cups graham cracker crumbs
¼ cup sugar
⅓ cup (⅔ stick) butter or margarine, melted
2 (8-ounce) packages cream cheese, softened
1 (14-ounce) can EAGLE® BRAND Sweetened Condensed
    Milk (NOT evaporated milk)
3 eggs
¼ cup REALEMON® Lemon Juice From Concentrate
1 (8-ounce) container sour cream, at room temperature
Raspberry Topping (recipe follows, optional)

1. Preheat oven to 300°F. Combine crumbs, sugar and butter; press firmly on bottom of ungreased 9-inch springform pan.

2. In large bowl, beat cream cheese until fluffy.

3. Gradually beat in **Eagle Brand** until smooth. Add eggs and **ReaLemon;** mix well. Pour into prepared pan. Bake 50 to 55 minutes or until set.

4. Remove from oven; top with sour cream. Bake 5 minutes longer. Cool 1 hour. Chill at least 4 hours. Prepare Raspberry Topping and serve with cheesecake. Store covered in refrigerator.

Makes 1 (9-inch) cheesecake

Raspberry Topping

Prep Time: 5 minutes

1 (10-ounce) package thawed frozen red raspberries in
    syrup
¼ cup red current jelly or red raspberry jam
1 tablespoon cornstarch

1. Drain ⅔ cup syrup from raspberries.

2. In small saucepan over medium heat, combine syrup, jelly and cornstarch. Cook and stir until slightly thickened and clear. Cool. Stir in raspberries.

New York Style Cheesecake: Increase cream cheese to 4 (8-ounce) packages and eggs to 4. Proceed as directed, adding 2 tablespoons flour after eggs. Bake 1 hour 10 minutes or until center is set. Omit sour cream. Cool. Chill. Serve and store as directed.

Blueberry Streusel Cobbler

Prep Time: 15 minutes   Bake Time: 1 hour and 10 minutes

1 pint fresh or frozen blueberries
1 (14-ounce) can EAGLE® BRAND Sweetened Condensed
  Milk (NOT evaporated milk)
2 teaspoons grated lemon peel
¾ cup (1½ sticks) plus 2 tablespoons cold butter or
  margarine, divided
 2 cups biscuit baking mix, divided
½ cup firmly packed brown sugar
½ cup chopped nuts
  Vanilla ice cream
  Blueberry Sauce (recipe follows)

1. Preheat oven to 325°F. In bowl, combine blueberries, **Eagle Brand** and peel.

2. In large bowl, cut ¾ cup butter into 1½ cups biscuit mix until crumbly; add blueberry mixture. Spread in greased 9-inch square baking pan.

3. In small bowl, combine remaining ½ cup biscuit mix and sugar; cut in remaining 2 tablespoons butter until crumbly. Add nuts. Sprinkle over cobbler.

4. Bake 1 hour and 10 minutes or until golden. Serve warm with vanilla ice cream and Blueberry Sauce. Refrigerate leftovers.

Makes 8 to 12 servings

Blueberry Sauce: In saucepan, combine ½ cup sugar, 1 tablespoon cornstarch, ½ teaspoon ground cinnamon and ¼ teaspoon ground nutmeg. Gradually add ½ cup water. Cook and stir until thickened. Stir in 1 pint blueberries; cook and stir until hot. Makes about 1⅔ cups.

Blueberry Streusel Cobbler

Walnut Rum Raisin Cheesecake

Prep Time: 20 minutes   Bake Time: 55 to 60 minutes

     1 cup raisins
     2 tablespoons rum or water plus ½ teaspoon rum flavoring
     1 cup graham cracker crumbs
     ½ cup finely chopped walnuts
     ¼ cup sugar
     ¼ cup (½ stick) butter or margarine, melted
     3 (8-ounce) packages cream cheese, softened
     1 (14-ounce) can EAGLE® BRAND Sweetened Condensed
        Milk (NOT evaporated milk)
     3 eggs
        Walnut Praline Glaze (recipe follows)

1. Preheat oven to 300°F. In small bowl, combine raisins and rum; set aside.

2. Combine graham cracker crumbs, nuts, sugar and butter; press firmly on bottom of 9-inch springform pan or 13×9-inch baking pan.

3. In large mixing bowl, beat cheese until fluffy. Gradually beat in **Eagle Brand** until smooth. Add eggs; mix well. Drain rum from raisins; stir rum into batter. Pour into prepared pan. Top evenly with raisins.

4. Bake 55 to 60 minutes or until center is set. Cool. Top with Walnut Praline Glaze. Chill. Refrigerate leftovers.

Makes 1 (9-inch) cheesecake

Walnut Praline Glaze: In small saucepan, combine ⅓ cup firmly packed dark brown sugar and ⅓ cup whipping cream. Cook and stir until sugar dissolves. Bring to a boil; reduce heat and simmer 5 minutes or until thickened. Remove from heat; stir in ¾ cup chopped toasted walnuts. Spoon over cake. (For 13×9-inch pan, double all glaze ingredients; simmer 10 to 12 minutes or until thickened.)

Fudge Ribbon Sheet Cake

Prep Time: 10 minutes   Bake Time: 20 minutes

1 (18¼-ounce) package chocolate cake mix
1 (8-ounce) package cream cheese, softened
2 tablespoons butter or margarine, softened
1 tablespoon cornstarch
1 (14-ounce) can EAGLE® BRAND Sweetened Condensed
    Milk (NOT evaporated milk)
1 egg
1 teaspoon vanilla extract
    Chocolate Glaze (recipe follows)

1. Preheat oven to 350°F. Grease and flour 15×10-inch jelly-roll pan. Prepare cake mix as package directs. Pour batter into prepared pan.

2. In small bowl, beat cream cheese, butter and cornstarch until fluffy. Gradually beat in **Eagle Brand**. Add egg and vanilla; beat until smooth. Spoon evenly over cake batter.

3. Bake 20 minutes or until toothpick inserted near center comes out clean. Cool. Prepare Chocolate Glaze and drizzle over cake. Store covered in refrigerator.   *Makes 10 to 12 servings*

Chocolate Glaze: In small saucepan over low heat, melt 1 (1-ounce) square unsweetened or semi-sweet chocolate and 1 tablespoon butter or margarine with 2 tablespoons water. Remove from heat. Stir in ¾ cup powdered sugar and ½ teaspoon vanilla extract. Stir until smooth and well blended.

Fudge Ribbon Bundt Cake: Preheat oven to 350°F. Grease and flour 10-inch bundt pan. Prepare cake mix as package directs. Pour batter into prepared pan. Prepare cream cheese topping as directed above; spoon evenly over batter. Bake 50 to 55 minutes or until toothpick inserted near center comes out clean. Cool 10 minutes. Remove from pan. Cool. Prepare Chocolate Glaze and drizzle over cake. Store covered in refrigerator.

IT TAKES THE CAKE

Frozen Mocha Cheesecake Loaf

Prep Time: 20 minutes   Freeze Time: 6 hours

**2 cups finely crushed crème-filled chocolate sandwich
  cookies (about 20 cookies)**
3 tablespoons butter or margarine, melted
1 (8-ounce) package cream cheese, softened
**1 (14-ounce) can EAGLE® BRAND Sweetened Condensed
  Milk (NOT evaporated milk)**
1 tablespoon vanilla extract
2 cups (1 pint) whipping cream, whipped
**2 tablespoons instant coffee dissolved in 1 tablespoon hot
  water**
½ cup chocolate-flavored syrup

1. Line 9×5-inch loaf pan with foil, extending foil above sides of pan. Combine cookie crumbs and butter; press firmly on bottom and halfway up sides of prepared pan.

2. In large mixing bowl, beat cream cheese until fluffy. Gradually add **Eagle Brand** until smooth; add vanilla.

3. Fold in whipped cream. Remove half the mixture and place in medium bowl; fold in coffee liquid and chocolate syrup. Spoon half the chocolate mixture into prepared pan then half the vanilla mixture. Repeat. With table knife, cut through cream mixture to marble.

4. Cover; freeze 6 hours or until firm. To serve, remove from pan; peel off foil. Garnish as desired. Slice to serve. Freeze leftovers.

Makes 8 to 10 servings

Frozen Mocha Cheesecake Loaf

Kids in the Kitchen

Cookie Pizza

Prep Time: 15 minutes   Bake Time: 14 minutes

1 (18-ounce) roll refrigerated sugar cookie dough
2 cups (12 ounces) semi-sweet chocolate chips
1 (14-ounce) can EAGLE® BRAND Sweetened Condensed
    Milk (NOT evaporated milk)
2 cups candy-coated milk chocolate candies
2 cups miniature marshmallows
½ cup peanuts

1. Preheat oven 375°F. Press cookie dough into 2 ungreased 12-inch pizza pans. Bake 10 minutes or until golden. Remove from oven.

2. In medium-sized saucepan, melt chips with **Eagle Brand**. Spread over crusts. Sprinkle with milk chocolate candies, marshmallows and peanuts.

3. Bake 4 minutes or until marshmallows are lightly toasted. Cool. Cut into wedges.   *Makes 2 pizzas (24 servings)*

Golden Peanut Butter Bars

Prep Time: 20 minutes   Bake Time: 40 minutes

2 cups all-purpose flour
¾ cup firmly packed light brown sugar
1 egg, beaten
½ cup (1 stick) cold butter or margarine
1 cup finely chopped peanuts
1 (14-ounce) can EAGLE® BRAND Sweetened Condensed
   Milk (NOT evaporated milk)
½ cup peanut butter
1 teaspoon vanilla extract

1. Preheat oven to 350°F. Combine flour, sugar and egg in large bowl; cut in cold butter until crumbly. Stir in peanuts. Reserving 2 cups crumb mixture, press remaining mixture on bottom of 13×9-inch baking pan.

2. Bake 15 minutes or until lightly browned.

3. Meanwhile, beat **Eagle Brand**, peanut butter and vanilla in another large bowl. Spread over prepared crust; top with reserved crumb mixture.

4. Bake an additional 25 minutes or until lightly browned. Cool. Cut into bars. Store covered at room temperature.

Makes 24 to 36 bars

Golden Peanut Butter Bars

KIDS IN THE KITCHEN

Candy Crunch

Prep Time: 15 minutes   Chill Time: 1 to 2 hours

4 cups (half of 15-ounce bag) pretzel sticks or pretzel twists
1 (14-ounce) can EAGLE® BRAND Sweetened Condensed Milk (NOT evaporated milk)
2 (10- to 12-ounce) bags white baking pieces
1 cup dried fruit, such as dried cranberries, raisins or mixed dried fruit bits

1. Line 15×10-inch baking pan with foil. Place pretzels in large bowl.

2. In large saucepan, over medium-low heat, heat **Eagle Brand** until warm, about 5 minutes. Remove from heat and immediately stir in white baking pieces until melted. Pour over pretzels, stirring to coat.

3. Immediately spread mixture into prepared pan. Sprinkle with dried fruit; press down lightly with back of spoon.

4. Chill 1 to 2 hours or until set. Break into chunks. Store loosely covered at room temperature.   *Makes about 1¾ pounds*

 *Helpful Hint*

> *To measure Eagle Brand, remove entire lid and scrape the Eagle Brand into a glass measuring cup using a rubber scraper.*

Creamy Banana Pudding

Prep Time: 15 minutes

1 (14-ounce) can EAGLE® BRAND Sweetened Condensed
   Milk (NOT evaporated milk)
1½ cups cold water
1 (4-serving size) package instant vanilla flavor pudding
   mix
2 cups (1 pint) whipping cream, whipped
36 vanilla wafers
3 medium bananas, sliced and dipped in REALEMON®
   Lemon Juice from Concentrate

1. In large mixing bowl, combine **Eagle Brand** and water. Add pudding mix; beat until well blended. Chill 5 minutes.

2. Fold in whipped cream. Spoon 1 cup pudding mixture into 2½-quart glass serving bowl.

3. Top with one-third each the vanilla wafers, bananas and pudding. Repeat layering twice, ending with pudding mixture. Chill thoroughly. Garnish as desired. Refrigerate leftovers.

Makes 8 to 10 servings

 *Helpful Hint*

For festive individual pudding desserts for your holiday guests, prepare mixture and layer in individual serving dessert dishes or cups with stems. Serve chilled.

KIDS IN THE KITCHEN

Golden Snacking Granola

Prep Time: 15 minutes   Bake Time: 55 to 60 minutes

2 cups oats
1½ cups silvered almonds or coarsely chopped walnuts
1 (3½-ounce) can flaked coconut (1⅓ cups)
½ cup sunflower seeds
½ cup wheat germ
2 tablespoons sesame seeds
1 teaspoon ground cinnamon
1 teaspoon salt
1 (14-ounce) can EAGLE® BRAND Sweetened Condensed Milk (NOT evaporated milk)
¼ cup vegetable oil
1 cup banana chips (optional)
1 cup raisins

1. Preheat oven to 300°F.

2. In large mixing bowl, combine all ingredients except banana chips and raisins; mix well.

3. Spread evenly in aluminum foil-lined 15×10-inch jelly-roll pan or baking sheet.

4. Bake 55 to 60 minutes, stirring every 15 minutes. Remove from oven; stir in banana chips and raisins.

5. Cool thoroughly. Store tightly covered at room temperature.

Makes about 2½ quarts

Prize Cookies

Prep Time: 15 minutes   Bake Time: 8 to 10 minutes

1½ **cups sugar**
  1 **cup shortening**
  3 **eggs**
  3 **cups all-purpose flour**
  1 **teaspoon baking soda**
½ **teaspoon salt**
  1 **(9-ounce) package NONE SUCH® Condensed Mincemeat,**
     crumbled

1. Preheat oven to 375°F. In large mixing bowl, beat sugar and shortening until fluffy. Add eggs; beat well. Stir together dry ingredients; gradually add to shortening mixture. Mix well. Stir in **None Such**.

2. Drop by rounded teaspoonfuls, 2 inches apart, onto greased baking sheets.

3. Bake 8 to 10 minutes or until lightly browned. Cool. Frost, if desired.

Makes about 6½ dozen cookies

 *Helpful Hint*

For a more cake-like cookie, substitute 1⅓ cups (one-half 27-ounce jar) **None Such®** Ready-to-Use Mincemeat (Regular or Brandy & Rum) for condensed mincemeat.

KIDS IN THE KITCHEN

S'Mores on a Stick

Prep Time: 10 minutes   Cook Time: 3 minutes

1 (14-ounce) can EAGLE® BRAND Sweetened Condensed Milk (NOT evaporated milk), divided
1½ cups milk chocolate mini chips, divided
1 cup miniature marshmallows
11 whole graham crackers, halved crosswise
Toppings: chopped peanuts, candy-coated chocolate mini pieces, sprinkles

1. Microwave half of **Eagle Brand** in microwave-safe bowl at HIGH (100% power) 1½ minutes. Stir in 1 cup chocolate chips until smooth; stir in marshmallows.

2. Spread evenly by heaping tablespoonfuls onto 11 graham cracker halves. Top with remaining graham cracker halves; place on waxed paper.

3. Microwave remaining **Eagle Brand** at HIGH (100% power) 1½ minutes; stir in remaining ½ cup chocolate chips, stirring until smooth. Drizzle mixture over cookies and sprinkle with desired toppings.

4. Let stand for 2 hours; insert a wooden craft stick in center of each cookie.   *Makes 11 servings*

S'Mores on a Stick

Banana Smoothies & Pops

Prep Time: 5 minutes

1 (14-ounce) can EAGLE® BRAND Sweetened Condensed Milk (NOT evaporated milk)
1 (8-ounce) container vanilla yogurt
2 ripe bananas
½ cup orange juice

Process **Eagle Brand** and remaining ingredients in blender until smooth, stopping to scrape down sides. Serve immediately.

Makes 4 cups

Fruit Smoothies: Substitute 1 cup of your favorite fruit and ½ cup any fruit juice for banana and orange juice.

Banana Smoothie Pops: Spoon banana mixture into 8 (5-ounce) paper cups. Freeze 30 minutes. Insert wooden craft sticks into the center of each cup; freeze until firm. Makes 8 pops.

 *Helpful Hint*

Use leftover Eagle Brand as a topper for waffles and French toast or stir some into coffee or tea for a coffeehouse-type beverage.

Banana Smoothie & Pops

Bite-Size Wonders

Chocolate Peanut Butter Chip Cookies

Prep Time: 15 minutes   Bake Time: 6 to 8 minutes

8 (1-ounce) squares semi-sweet chocolate
3 tablespoons butter or margarine
1 (14-ounce) can EAGLE® BRAND Sweetened Condensed
    Milk (NOT evaporated milk)
2 cups biscuit baking mix
1 teaspoon vanilla extract
1 cup (6 ounces) peanut butter-flavored chips

1. Preheat oven to 350°F. In large saucepan, over low heat, melt chocolate and butter with **Eagle Brand**; remove from heat. Add biscuit mix and vanilla; with mixer, beat until smooth and well blended.

2. Let mixture cool to room temperature. Stir in chips. Shape into 1¼-inch balls. Place 2 inches apart on ungreased baking sheets. Bake 6 to 8 minutes or until tops are lightly crusty. Cool. Store tightly covered at room temperature.   *Makes about 4 dozen cookies*

MAKE MAGIC IN MINUTES

Chocolate Chip Treasure Cookies

Prep Time: 15 minutes   Bake Time: 9 to 10 minutes

- 1½ cups graham cracker crumbs
- ½ cup all-purpose flour
- 2 teaspoons baking powder
- 1 (14-ounce) can EAGLE® BRAND Sweetened Condensed Milk (NOT evaporated milk)
- ½ cup (1 stick) butter or margarine, softened
- 1⅓ cups flaked coconut
- 2 cups (12 ounces) semi-sweet chocolate chips
- 1 cup chopped walnuts or miniature candy-coated chocolate pieces

1. Preheat oven to 375°F. In medium bowl, combine graham cracker crumbs, flour and baking powder.

2. In large bowl, beat **Eagle Brand** and butter until smooth. Add crumb mixture; mix well. Stir in coconut, chips and walnuts or miniature candy-coated chocolate pieces.

3. Drop by rounded tablespoonfuls onto ungreased cookie sheets. Bake 9 to 10 minutes or until lightly browned. Cool. Store loosely covered at room temperature.   *Makes about 4 dozen cookies*

 *Helpful Hint*

Homemade treats become gorgeous gifts when arranged in unique packages wrapped in festive papers and decorated with ribbons or bows.

BITE-SIZE WONDERS

Fruit Bon Bons

Prep Time: 20 minutes   Chill Time: 1 hour

1 (14-ounce) can EAGLE® BRAND Sweetened Condensed
   Milk (NOT evaporated milk)
2 (7-ounce) packages flaked coconut (5⅓ cups)
1 (6-ounce) package fruit flavor gelatin, any flavor, divided
1 cup ground blanched almonds
1 teaspoon almond extract
   Food coloring (optional)

1. In large mixing bowl, combine **Eagle Brand**, coconut, ⅓ cup
gelatin, almonds, extract and enough food coloring to tint mixture
desired shade. Chill 1 hour or until firm enough to handle.

2. Using about ½ tablespoon mixture for each, shape into 1-inch
balls. Sprinkle remaining gelatin onto wax paper; roll each ball in
gelatin to coat.

3. Place on waxed-paper-lined baking sheets; chill.

4. Store covered at room temperature or in refrigerator.

Makes about 5 dozen bon bons

 *Helpful Hint*

Show someone how much you care by wrapping delicious
Eagle Brand treats in fun festive containers, such as
baskets, boxes and tins.

Peppermint Chocolate Fudge

Prep Time: 10 minutes   Chill Time: 2 hours

1 (12-ounce) package milk chocolate chips (2 cups)
1 cup (6 ounces) semi-sweet chocolate chips
1 (14-ounce) can EAGLE® BRAND Sweetened Condensed
 Milk (NOT evaporated milk)
 Dash salt
½ teaspoon peppermint extract
¼ cup crushed hard peppermint candy

1. In saucepan, over low heat, melt chips with **Eagle Brand** and salt. Remove from heat; stir in extract. Spread evenly into foil-lined 8- or 9-inch square pan. Sprinkle with peppermint candy.

2. Chill 2 hours or until firm. Turn fudge onto cutting board; peel off foil and cut into squares. Store loosely covered at room temperature.

Makes about 2 pounds

 *Helpful Hint*

Clean-up will be a snap if you line the entire pan with foil before adding cookie batter or fudge. When cool, lift the edges of the foil to remove the block from the pan. Cut the block into squares, diamonds or rectangles.

Peppermint Chocolate Fudge and
Chocolate Snowswirl Fudge (page 84)

BITE-SIZE WONDERS

Peanut Butter Blocks

Prep Time: 15 minutes   Chill Time: 2 hours

1 (14-ounce) can **EAGLE® BRAND Sweetened Condensed Milk (NOT evaporated milk)**
1¼ cups creamy peanut butter
⅓ cup water
1 tablespoon vanilla extract
½ teaspoon salt
1 cup cornstarch, sifted
1 pound vanilla-flavored candy coating*
2 cups peanuts, finely chopped

Also called confectionery coating or almond bark.

1. In heavy saucepan, combine **Eagle Brand**, peanut butter, water, vanilla and salt; stir in cornstarch. Over medium heat, cook and stir until thickened and smooth.

2. Add candy coating; cook and stir until melted and smooth. Spread evenly in waxed-paper-lined 9-inch square pan. Chill 2 hours or until firm. Cut into squares; roll firmly in peanuts to coat. Store covered at room temperature or in refrigerator.   *Makes about 3 pounds*

Microwave Method: In 1-quart glass measure, combine **Eagle Brand**, peanut butter, water, vanilla and salt; stir in cornstarch. Microwave at HIGH (100% power) 2 minutes; mix well. In microwavable 2-quart glass measure, melt candy coating at MEDIUM (50% power) 3 to 5 minutes, stirring after each minute. Add peanut butter mixture; mix well. Proceed as directed above.

Foolproof Chocolate Fudge

Prep Time: 10 minutes   Chill Time: 2 hours

3 (6-ounce) packages semi-sweet chocolate chips
1 (14-ounce) can EAGLE® BRAND Sweetened Condensed
      Milk (NOT evaporated milk)
   Dash salt
½ to 1 cup chopped nuts (optional)
1½ teaspoons vanilla extract

1. Line 8- or 9-inch square pan with foil. Butter foil; set aside.

2. In heavy saucepan over low heat, melt chips with **Eagle Brand** and salt. Remove from heat; stir in nuts, if desired, and vanilla. Spread evenly in prepared pan.

3. Chill 2 hours or until firm. Turn fudge onto cutting board; peel off foil and cut into squares. Store covered in refrigerator.

Makes about 2 pounds

Marshmallow Fudge: Stir in 2 tablespoons butter with vanilla. Substitute 2 cups miniature marshmallows for nuts. Proceed as directed above.

BITE-SIZE WONDERS

Choco-Peanut Pinwheels

Prep Time: 15 minutes   Chill Time: 2 hours

1 cup (6 ounces) peanut butter-flavored chips
1 (14-ounce) can EAGLE® BRAND Sweetened Condensed
**   Milk (NOT evaporated milk), divided**
1 cup (6 ounces) semi-sweet chocolate chips
1 teaspoon vanilla extract

1. Cut waxed paper into 15×10-inch rectangle; butter paper.

2. In heavy saucepan, over low heat, melt peanut butter chips with ²/₃ cup **Eagle Brand**. Cool slightly. With fingers, press evenly into thin layer to cover waxed paper. Let stand at room temperature 15 minutes.

3. In heavy saucepan, melt chocolate chips with remaining **Eagle Brand**. Remove from heat; stir in vanilla. Spread evenly over peanut butter layer. Let stand at room temperature 30 minutes.

4. Beginning at 15-inch side, roll up tightly, jelly-roll fashion, without waxed paper. Wrap tightly in plastic wrap.

5. Chill 2 hours or until firm. Cut into ¼-inch slices to serve. Store covered at room temperature.   *Makes about 1½ pounds*

Choco-Peanut Pinwheels

BITE-SIZE WONDERS

The Best Bar in Town

Cheesecake-Topped Brownies

Prep Time: 20 minutes   Bake Time: 40 to 45 minutes

1 (21- or 23.6-ounce) package fudge brownie mix
1 (8-ounce) package cream cheese, softened
2 tablespoons butter or margarine, softened
1 tablespoon cornstarch
1 (14-ounce) can EAGLE® BRAND Sweetened Condensed
    Milk (NOT evaporated milk)
1 egg
2 teaspoons vanilla extract
    Ready-to-spread chocolate frosting (optional)
    Orange peel (optional)

1. Preheat oven to 350°F. Prepare brownie mix as package directs. Spread into well-greased 13×9-inch baking pan.

2. In large mixing bowl, beat cream cheese, butter and cornstarch until fluffy.

3. Gradually beat in **Eagle Brand.** Add egg and vanilla; beat until smooth. Pour cheesecake mixture evenly over brownie batter.

4. Bake 40 to 45 minutes or until top is lightly browned. Cool. Spread with frosting or sprinkle with orange peel, if desired. Cut into bars. Store covered in refrigerator.   *Makes 36 to 40 bars*

Double Delicious Cookie Bars

Prep Time: 10 minutes   Bake Time: 25 to 30 minutes

½ cup (1 stick) butter or margarine
1½ cups graham cracker crumbs
**1 (14-ounce) can EAGLE® BRAND Sweetened Condensed
      Milk (NOT evaporated milk)**
2 cups (12 ounces) semi-sweet chocolate chips*
1 cup (6 ounces) peanut butter-flavored chips*

Butterscotch-flavored or white chocolate chips may be substituted for the semi-sweet chocolate and/or peanut butter chips.

1. Preheat oven to 350°F.

2. In 13×9-inch baking pan, melt butter in oven. Sprinkle crumbs evenly over butter; pour **Eagle Brand** evenly over crumbs. Top with remaining ingredients; press down firmly.

3. Bake 25 to 30 minutes or until lightly browned. Cool. Cut into bars. Store covered at room temperature.   *Makes 24 to 36 bars*

Buckeye Cookie Bars

Prep Time: 20 minutes   Bake Time: 25 to 30 minutes

1 (18¼-ounce) package chocolate cake mix
¼ cup vegetable oil
1 egg
1 cup chopped peanuts
**1 (14-ounce) can EAGLE® BRAND Sweetened Condensed
      Milk (NOT evaporated milk)**
½ cup peanut butter

1. Preheat oven to 350°F.

2. In large mixing bowl, combine cake mix, oil and egg; beat on medium speed until crumbly. Stir in peanuts. Reserve 1½ cups crumb mixture; press remaining mixture firmly on bottom of greased 13×9-inch baking pan.

3. In medium bowl, beat **Eagle Brand** with peanut butter until smooth; spread over prepared crust. Sprinkle with reserved crumb mixture.

4. Bake 25 to 30 minutes or until set. Cool. Cut into bars. Store loosely covered at room temperature.   *Makes 24 to 36 bars*

Lemony Cheesecake Bars

Prep Time: 25 minutes   Bake Time: 35 minutes

1½ **cups graham cracker crumbs**
⅓ **cup finely chopped pecans**
⅓ **cup sugar**
⅓ **cup (⅔ stick) melted butter or margarine**
2 **(8-ounce) packages cream cheese, softened**
1 **(14-ounce) can EAGLE® BRAND Sweetened Condensed Milk (NOT evaporated milk)**
2 **eggs**
½ **cup REALEMON® Lemon Juice from Concentrate**

1. Preheat oven to 325°F. Combine graham cracker crumbs, pecans, sugar and melted butter in mixing bowl. Reserve ⅓ cup; press remaining mixture into 13×9-inch baking pan. Bake 5 minutes. Remove and cool on wire rack.

2. Beat cream cheese in large mixing bowl until fluffy. Gradually beat in **Eagle Brand**. Add eggs; beat until just combined. Stir in **ReaLemon**. Carefully spoon mixture onto crust in pan. Spoon reserved crumb mixture to make diagonal stripes on top of cheese mixture or sprinkle to cover.

3. Bake about 30 minutes or until knife inserted near center comes out clean. Cool on wire rack 1 hour. Store in refrigerator. Cut into bars and serve.   *Makes 36 bars*

Chocolate Nut Bars

Prep Time: 10 minutes   Bake Time: 33 to 38 minutes

1¾ cups graham cracker crumbs
½ cup (1 stick) butter or margarine, melted
1 (14-ounce) can EAGLE® BRAND Sweetened Condensed Milk (NOT evaporated milk)
2 cups (12 ounces) semi-sweet chocolate chips, divided
1 teaspoon vanilla extract
1 cup chopped nuts

1. Preheat oven to 375°F. Combine crumbs and butter; press firmly on bottom of 13×9-inch baking pan. Bake 8 minutes. *Reduce oven temperature to 350°F.*

2. In small saucepan, melt **Eagle Brand** with 1 cup chocolate chips and vanilla. Spread chocolate mixture over prepared crust. Top with remaining 1 cup chocolate chips then nuts; press down firmly.

3. Bake 25 to 30 minutes. Cool. Chill if desired. Cut into bars. Store loosely covered at room temperature.   *Makes 24 to 36 bars*

Chocolate Nut Bars

Lemon Crumb Bars

Prep Time: 30 minutes   Bake Time: 35 minutes

1 (18¼-ounce) package lemon or yellow cake mix
½ cup (1 stick) butter or margarine, softened
1 egg plus 3 egg yolks
2 cups (¼ pound) finely crushed saltine crackers
1 (14-ounce) can EAGLE® BRAND Sweetened Condensed
    Milk (NOT evaporated milk)
½ cup REALEMON® Lemon Juice From Concentrate

1. Preheat oven to 350°F. Grease 15×10×1-inch baking pan. In large bowl, combine cake mix, butter and 1 egg; mix well (mixture will be crumbly). Stir in cracker crumbs. Reserve 2 cups crumb mixture. Press remaining crumb mixture firmly on bottom of prepared pan. Bake 15 minutes.

2. Meanwhile, in medium bowl, combine egg yolks, **Eagle Brand** and **ReaLemon;** mix well. Spread evenly over baked crust.

3. Top with reserved crumb mixture. Bake 20 minutes or until firm. Cool. Cut into bars. Store covered in refrigerator.

Makes 36 to 48 bars

Marbled Cheesecake Bars

Prep Time: 20 minutes   Bake Time: 45 to 50 minutes

2 cups finely crushed créme-filled chocolate sandwich
    cookies (about 24 cookies)
3 tablespoons butter or margarine, melted
3 (8-ounce) packages cream cheese, softened
1 (14-ounce) can EAGLE® BRAND Sweetened Condensed
    Milk (NOT evaporated milk)
3 eggs
2 teaspoons vanilla extract
2 (1-ounce) squares unsweetened chocolate, melted

1. Preheat oven to 300°F. Combine cookie crumbs and butter; press firmly on bottom of ungreased 13×9-inch baking pan.

2. In large bowl, beat cream cheese until fluffy. Gradually beat in **Eagle Brand** until smooth. Add eggs and vanilla; mix well. Pour half the batter evenly over prepared crust.

3. Stir melted chocolate into remaining batter; spoon over vanilla batter. With table knife or metal spatula, gently swirl through batter to marble.

4. Bake 45 to 50 minutes or until set. Cool. Chill. Cut into bars. Store covered in refrigerator. *Makes 24 to 36 bars*

Helpful Hint: For best distribution of added ingredients (chocolate chips, nuts, etc.) or for even marbling, do not oversoften or overbeat the cream cheese.

Fudgy Chocolate Pecan Bars
Prep Time: 20 minutes   Bake Time: 50 minutes

  1 **cup unsifted flour**
⅔ **cup sugar**
½ **cup unsweetened cocoa powder**
½ **teaspoon salt**
¾ **cup (1½ sticks) cold butter or margarine**
  2 **eggs, divided**
  1 **(14-ounce) can EAGLE® BRAND Sweetened Condensed Milk (NOT evaporated milk)**
1½ **teaspoons maple flavoring**
  2 **cups pecan halves or pieces**

1. Preheat oven to 350°F. In large bowl, combine flour, sugar, cocoa and salt; cut in cold butter until crumbly. Stir in 1 beaten egg. Press evenly into 13×9-inch baking pan.

2. Bake 25 minutes. Meanwhile, in medium bowl, beat in **Eagle Brand**, remaining 1 egg and flavoring; stir in pecan halves. Pour over baked crust, distributing pecan halves evenly.

3. Bake 25 minutes longer or until golden. Cut into bars. Store tightly covered at room temperature. *Makes 24 to 36 bars*

THE BEST BAR IN TOWN

Magic Cookie Bars

Prep Time: 10 minutes   Bake Time: 25 minutes

½ cup (1 stick) butter or margarine
1½ cups graham cracker crumbs
1 (14-ounce) can EAGLE® BRAND Sweetened Condensed Milk (NOT evaporated milk)
2 cups (12 ounces) semi-sweet chocolate chips
1⅓ cups flaked coconut
1 cup chopped nuts

1. Preheat oven to 350°F. In 13×9-inch baking pan, melt butter in oven.

2. Sprinkle crumbs over butter; pour **Eagle Brand** evenly over graham cracker crumbs. Top with remaining ingredients; press down firmly with fork.

3. Bake 25 minutes or until lightly browned. Cool. Chill, if desired. Cut into bars. Store loosely covered at room temperature.

Makes 24 to 36 bars

7-Layer Magic Cookie Bars: Substitute 1 cup (6 ounces) butterscotch-flavored chips* for 1 cup semi-sweet chocolate chips and proceed as directed above.

*Peanut butter-flavored chips or white chocolate chips may be substituted for butterscotch-flavored chips.

Magic Peanut Cookie Bars: Substitute 2 cups (about ¾ pound) chocolate-covered peanuts for semi-sweet chocolate chips and chopped nuts.

Magic Rainbow Cookie Bars: Substitute 2 cups plain candy-coated chocolate pieces for semi-sweet chocolate chips.

Magic Cookie Bars

THE BEST BAR IN TOWN

Toffee-Top Cheesecake Bars

Prep Time: 20 minutes   Bake Time: 40 minutes
Cool Time: 15 minutes

1¼ **cups all-purpose flour**
1 **cup powdered sugar**
½ **cup unsweetened cocoa powder**
¼ **teaspoon baking soda**
¾ **cup (1½ sticks) butter or margarine**
1 **(8-ounce) package cream cheese, softened**
1 **(14-ounce) can EAGLE® BRAND Sweetened Condensed**
    Milk (NOT evaporated milk)
2 **eggs**
1 **teaspoon vanilla extract**
1½ **cups (8-ounce package) English toffee bits, divided**

1. Heat oven 350°F. Combine flour, powdered sugar, cocoa and baking soda in medium bowl; cut in butter until mixture is crumbly. Press into bottom of ungreased 13×9-inch baking pan. Bake 15 minutes.

2. Beat cream cheese until fluffy. Add **Eagle Brand**, eggs and vanilla; beat until smooth. Stir in 1 cup English toffee bits. Pour mixture over hot crust. Bake 25 minutes or until set and edges just begin to brown.

3. Remove from oven. Cool 15 minutes. Sprinkle remaining ¾ cup English toffee bits evenly over top. Cool completely. Refrigerate several hours or until cold. Store leftovers covered in refrigerator.

Makes about 36 bars

Toffee-Top Cheesecake Bars

Sweetie Pies

Sweet Potato Pecan Pie
Prep Time: 30 minutes   Bake Time: 45 minutes

1 pound sweet potatoes or yams, cooked and peeled
¼ cup (½ stick) butter or margarine, softened
1 (14-ounce) can EAGLE® BRAND Sweetened Condensed
**   Milk (NOT evaporated milk)**
1 teaspoon *each* ground cinnamon, grated orange peel and
**   vanilla extract**
½ teaspoon ground nutmeg
¼ teaspoon salt
1 egg
1 (6-ounce) graham cracker crumb pie crust
**   Pecan Topping (recipe follows)**

1. Preheat oven to 425°F. With mixer, beat hot sweet potatoes and butter until smooth. Add **Eagle Brand** and remaining ingredients except crust and Pecan Topping; mix well. Pour into crust.

2. Bake 20 minutes. Meanwhile, prepare Pecan Topping.

3. Remove pie from oven; *reduce oven temperature to 350°F.* Spoon Pecan Topping on pie.

4. Bake 25 minutes longer or until set. Cool. Serve warm or at room temperature. Garnish with orange zest twist, if desired. Refrigerate leftovers.   *Makes 1 pie*

Pecan Topping: Beat together 1 egg, 2 tablespoons each dark corn syrup and firmly packed brown sugar, 1 tablespoon melted butter and ½ teaspoon maple flavoring. Stir in 1 cup chopped pecans. (Use pecan topping mixture in recipe as noted above.)

Decadent Brownie Pie

Prep Time: 25 minutes   Bake Time: 45 to 50 minutes

1 (9-inch) unbaked pastry shell
1 cup (6 ounces) semi-sweet chocolate chips
¼ cup (½ stick) butter or margarine
1 (14-ounce) can EAGLE® BRAND Sweetened Condensed
    Milk (NOT evaporated milk)
½ cup biscuit baking mix
2 eggs
1 teaspoon vanilla extract
1 cup chopped nuts
  Vanilla ice cream

1. Preheat oven to 375°F. Bake pastry shell 10 minutes; remove from oven. *Reduce oven temperature to 325°F.*

2. In saucepan over low heat, melt chips with butter.

3. In mixing bowl, beat chocolate mixture with **Eagle Brand**, biscuit mix, eggs and vanilla until smooth. Add nuts. Pour into pastry shell.

4. Bake 35 to 40 minutes or until center is set. Serve warm or at room temperature with ice cream. Refrigerate leftovers.

Makes 1 (9-inch) pie

Decadent Brownie Pie

Key Lime Pie

Prep Time: 25 minutes   Bake Time: 45 minutes
Cool Time: 1 hour   Chill Time: 3 hours

3 eggs, separated
1 (14-ounce) can EAGLE® BRAND Sweetened Condensed
Milk (NOT evaporated milk)
½ cup REALIME® Lime Juice From Concentrate
2 to 3 drops green food coloring (optional)
1 (9-inch) unbaked pastry shell
½ teaspoon cream of tartar
⅓ cup sugar

1. Preheat oven to 325°F. In medium bowl, beat egg yolks; gradually beat in **Eagle Brand** and **ReaLime.** Stir in food coloring. Pour into pastry shell.

2. Bake 30 minutes. Remove from oven. *Increase oven temperature to 350°F.*

3. Meanwhile, for meringue, with clean mixer, beat egg whites and cream of tartar in large mixing bowl to soft peaks. Gradually beat in sugar, 1 tablespoon at a time. Beat 4 minutes or until stiff, glossy peaks form and sugar is dissolved.

4. Immediately spread meringue over hot pie, carefully sealing to edge of crust to prevent meringue from shrinking. Bake 15 minutes. Cool 1 hour. Chill at least 3 hours. Store covered in refrigerator.

Makes 8 servings

Microwave Caramel Nut Cream Pie

Prep Time: 25 minutes   Microwave Time: 16 to 22 minutes
Chill Time: 3 hours

1 (14-ounce) can EAGLE® BRAND Sweetened Condensed Milk (NOT evaporated milk)
1 cup chopped nuts
2 tablespoons milk
½ teaspoon ground cinnamon
1 cup (½ pint) whipping cream, whipped
1 (6-ounce) graham cracker crumb pie crust

1. Pour **Eagle Brand** into microwavable 2-quart glass measure; microwave at MEDIUM (50% power) 4 minutes, stirring briskly every 2 minutes until smooth. Microwave at LOW (30% power) 12 to 18 minutes or until very thick and caramel-colored, stirring briskly every 2 minutes until smooth.

2. Stir nuts, milk and cinnamon into warm caramelized milk; cool to room temperature. Fold in whipped cream. Pour into crust.

3. Chill 3 hours or until set. Garnish as desired. Refrigerate leftovers.

Makes 1 pie

 *Helpful Hint*

Eagle Brand is more than just a magic ingredient. You can drizzle it over ice cream or use it as a dipper for fresh fruits and biscuits. Pour it over hot oatmeal or add it to coffee, tea or cocoa instead of cream.

Apple Custard Tart

Prep Time: 10 minutes   Bake Time: 40 minutes
Cool Time: 1 hour   Chill Time: 4 hours

**1 folded refrigerated unbaked pie crust (one-half of
15-ounce package)**
1½ cups sour cream
**1 (14-ounce) can EAGLE® BRAND Sweetened Condensed
Milk (NOT evaporated milk)**
¼ cup thawed frozen apple juice concentrate
1 egg
1½ teaspoons vanilla extract
¼ teaspoon ground cinnamon
Apple Cinnamon Glaze (recipe follows)
2 medium all-purpose apples, cored, pared and thinly sliced
1 tablespoon butter or margarine

1. Let refrigerated pie crust stand at room temperature according to package directions. Preheat oven to 375°F. On floured surface, roll pie crust from center to edge, forming circle about 13 inches in diameter. Ease pastry into 11-inch tart pan with removable bottom. Trim pastry even with rim of pan. Place pan on baking sheet. Bake crust 15 minutes or until lightly golden.

2. Meanwhile with mixer, beat sour cream, **Eagle Brand**, juice concentrate, egg, vanilla and cinnamon in small bowl until smooth. Pour into prebaked pie crust. Bake 25 minutes or until center appears set when shaken. Cool 1 hour on wire rack. Prepare Apple Cinnamon Glaze.

3. In large skillet, cook apples in butter until tender-crisp. Arrange apples on top of tart; drizzle with Apple Cinnamon Glaze. Chill in refrigerator at least 4 hours. Store leftovers loosely covered in refrigerator.   *Makes 1 tart*

Apple Cinnamon Glaze: In small saucepan, combine ⅓ cup thawed frozen apple juice concentrate, 1 teaspoon cornstarch and ½ teaspoon ground cinnamon. Mix well. Cook and stir over low heat until thickened and bubbly.

Apple Custard Tart

Heavenly Chocolate Mousse Pie

Prep Time: 20 minutes   Chill Time: 15 minutes

4 (1-ounce) squares unsweetened chocolate, melted
1 (14-ounce) can EAGLE® BRAND Sweetened Condensed
   Milk (NOT evaporated milk)
1½ teaspoons vanilla extract
1 cup (½ pint) whipping cream, whipped
1 (6-ounce) chocolate-flavored crumb pie crust

1. With mixer, beat chocolate with **Eagle Brand** and vanilla until well blended.

2. Chill 15 minutes until cooled; stir until smooth. Fold in whipped cream.

3. Pour into crust. Chill thoroughly. Garnish as desired. Refrigerate leftovers.   *Makes 1 pie*

 *Helpful Hint*

> *When there is little time to make pie crusts from scratch, the supermarket offers several work-saving options, from graham cracker and chocolate-flavored crumb crusts to refrigerated and frozen pastry shells.*

Heavenly Chocolate Mousse Pie

Fudgy Pecan Pie

Prep Time: 15 minutes   Bake Time: 40 to 45 minutes

2 (1-ounce) squares unsweetened chocolate
¼ cup (½ stick) butter or margarine
**1 (14-ounce) can EAGLE® BRAND Sweetened Condensed
     Milk (NOT evaporated milk)**
½ cup hot water
2 eggs, well beaten
1¼ cups pecan halves or pieces
1 teaspoon vanilla extract
⅛ teaspoon salt
1 (9-inch) unbaked pastry shell

1. Preheat oven to 350°F. In medium saucepan over low heat, melt chocolate and butter. Stir in **Eagle Brand**, hot water and eggs; mix well.

2. Remove from heat; stir in pecans, vanilla and salt. Pour into pastry shell. Bake 40 to 45 minutes or until center is set. Cool slightly. Serve warm or chilled. Garnish as desired. Store covered in refrigerator.

Makes 1 (9-inch) pie

Reduced-Fat Peppermint Pie

Prep Time: 20 minutes   Freeze Time: 6 hours

¼ **cup chocolate cookie crumbs**
1 **(8-ounce) package Neufchâtel cheese, softened**
1 **(14-ounce) can EAGLE® BRAND Fat Free Sweetened**
   Condensed Skimmed Milk (NOT evaporated milk)
1 **cup crushed hard peppermint candy**
   Red food coloring (optional)
1 **(8-ounce) container frozen non-dairy light whipped**
   topping, thawed

1. Spray 9-inch pie plate with nonstick cooking spray. Sprinkle cookie crumbs on side and bottom of plate.

2. Meanwhile, in large mixing bowl, beat Neufchâtel cheese until fluffy. Gradually beat in **Eagle Brand** until smooth. Stir in candy and food coloring, if desired.

3. Fold in whipped topping. Pour into prepared plate. Cover, freeze 6 hours or until firm. Garnish as desired. Freeze leftovers.

Makes 8 servings

Note: 50% less fat than the original recipe.

 *Helpful Hint*

If you want to trim the fat for any Eagle Brand recipe, just use **Eagle® Brand** *Fat Free or Low Fat Sweetened Condensed Milk instead of the original Eagle Brand.*

Frozen Peanut Butter Pie

Prep Time: 20 minutes   Freeze Time: 4 hours

Chocolate Crunch Crust (recipe follows)
1 (8-ounce) package cream cheese, softened
1 (14-ounce) can EAGLE® BRAND Sweetened Condensed
    Milk (NOT evaporated milk)
¾ cup peanut butter
2 tablespoons REALEMON® Lemon Juice from Concentrate
1 teaspoon vanilla extract
1 cup (½ pint) whipping cream, whipped
Chocolate fudge ice cream topping

1. Prepare Chocolate Crunch Crust. In large mixing bowl, beat cream cheese until fluffy; gradually beat in **Eagle Brand** then peanut butter until smooth. Stir in **ReaLemon** and vanilla.

2. Fold in whipped cream. Turn into prepared crust. Drizzle topping over pie. Freeze 4 hours or until firm. Return leftovers to freezer.

Makes 1 (9-inch) pie

Chocolate Crunch Crust: In heavy saucepan, over low heat, melt ⅓ cup butter or margarine and 1 (6-ounce) package semi-sweet chocolate chips. Remove from heat; gently stir in 2½ cups oven-toasted rice cereal until completely coated. Press on bottom and up side to rim of buttered 9-inch pie plate. Chill 30 minutes.

Frozen Peanut Butter Pie

Decadent Delights

Creamy Caramel Flan

Prep Time: 15 minutes   Bake Time: 25 minutes

¾ **cup sugar**
4 **eggs**
1¾ **cups water**
1 **(14-ounce) can EAGLE® BRAND Sweetened Condensed Milk (NOT evaporated milk)**
1 **teaspoon vanilla extract**
⅛ **teaspoon salt**
Sugar Garnish (recipe follows, optional)

1. Preheat oven to 350°F. In heavy skillet over medium heat, cook and stir sugar until melted and caramel-colored. Pour into 8 ungreased 6-ounce custard cups, tilting to coat bottoms.

2. In large bowl, beat eggs; stir in water, **Eagle Brand**, vanilla and salt. Pour into prepared custard cups. Set cups in large shallow pan. Fill pan with 1 inch hot water.

3. Bake 25 minutes or until knife inserted near centers comes out clean. Cool. Chill. To serve, invert 1 flan onto each serving plate. Top with Sugar Garnish or garnish as desired. Store covered in refrigerator.

Makes 8 servings

Sugar Garnish: Fill a medium-sized metal bowl half-full of ice. In medium-sized saucepan, combine 1 cup sugar with ¼ cup water. Stir; cover and bring to a boil. Cook over high heat 5 to 6 minutes or until light brown in color. Immediately put pan in ice for 1 minute. Using spoon, carefully drizzle sugar decoratively over foil. Cool. To serve, peel from foil.

No-Bake Fudgy Brownies

Prep Time: 10 minutes   Chill Time: 4 hours

1 (14-ounce) can **EAGLE® BRAND Sweetened Condensed Milk (NOT evaporated milk)**
2 (1-ounce) squares unsweetened chocolate, cut up
1 teaspoon vanilla extract
2 cups plus 2 tablespoons packaged chocolate cookie crumbs, divided
¼ cup miniature candy-coated milk chocolate candies or chopped nuts

1. Grease 8-inch square baking pan or line with foil; set aside.

2. In medium-sized heavy saucepan, combine **Eagle Brand** and chocolate; cook and stir over low heat just until boiling. Reduce heat; cook and stir for 2 to 3 minutes more or until mixture thickens. Remove from heat. Stir in vanilla.

3. Stir in 2 cups cookie crumbs. Spread evenly into prepared pan. Sprinkle with remaining cookie crumbs and candies or nuts; press down gently with back of spoon.

4. Cover and chill for 4 hours or until firm. Cut into squares. Store leftovers covered in refrigerator.   *Makes 24 to 36 bars*

No-Bake Fudgy Brownies

DECADENT DELIGHTS

Creamy Rice Pudding

Prep Time: 1 hour

2½ cups water
½ cup uncooked long grain rice
1 (3-inch) cinnamon stick or ¼ teaspoon ground cinnamon
2 (¼-inch) pieces lemon peel
Dash salt
1 (14-ounce) can EAGLE® BRAND Sweetened Condensed Milk (NOT evaporated milk)
Additional ground cinnamon

1. In medium saucepan combine water, rice, cinnamon, lemon peel and salt. Let mixture stand 30 minutes.

2. Bring mixture to a boil, stirring occasionally. Add **Eagle Brand**; mix well. Return to a boil; stir.

3. Reduce heat to medium. Cook uncovered, stirring frequently, 20 to 25 minutes or until liquid is absorbed to top of rice.

4. Cool. (Pudding thickens as it cools.) Remove cinnamon stick and lemon peel. Sprinkle with additional cinnamon. Serve warm or chilled. Refrigerate leftovers. *Makes 4 to 6 servings*

 *Helpful Hint*

> *Serve in decorative dessert cups or bowls for a more festive look at your next holiday gathering.*

Dulce de Leche

Prep Time: 5 minutes   Bake Time: 1 hour
Cool Time: 1 hour

1 (14-ounce) can EAGLE® BRAND Sweetened Condensed Milk (NOT evaporated milk)
Assorted dippers, such as cookies, cake, banana chunks, apple slices and/or strawberries

1. Preheat oven to 425°F. Pour **Eagle Brand** into 9-inch pie plate. Cover with foil; place in larger shallow baking pan. Pour hot water into larger pan to depth of 1 inch.

2. Bake 1 hour or until thick and caramel-colored. Beat until smooth. Cool 1 hour. Refrigerate until serving time. Serve as dip with assorted dippers. Store leftovers covered in refrigerator for up to 1 week.

Makes about 1 1/4 cups

CAUTION: Never heat an unopened can.

Mexican Coffee

Prep Time: 8 minutes

6 cups hot brewed coffee
1 (14-ounce) can EAGLE® BRAND Sweetened Condensed Milk (Original, Low Fat, or Fat Free) (NOT evaporated milk)
½ cup coffee liqueur
2 teaspoons vanilla extract
⅓ cup tequila (optional)
Ground cinnamon (optional)

Stir together first 4 ingredients and tequila, if desired. Sprinkle each serving with cinnamon, if desired.

Makes 8 cups

Creamy Cinnamon Rolls

Prep Time: 20 minutes   Bake Time: 30 to 35 minutes
Chill Time: Overnight   Cooling Time: 5 minutes

2 (1-pound) loaves frozen bread dough, thawed
⅔ cup (one-half 14-ounce) can EAGLE® BRAND Sweetened
    Condensed Milk* (NOT evaporated milk), divided
1 cup chopped pecans
2 teaspoons ground cinnamon
1 cup sifted powdered sugar
½ teaspoon vanilla extract
    Additional chopped pecans (optional)

** Use remaining **Eagle Brand** as a dip for fruit. Pour into storage container and store tightly covered in refrigerator for up to 1 week.*

1. On lightly floured surface roll each bread dough loaf into 12×9-inch rectangle. Spread ⅓ cup **Eagle Brand** over dough rectangles. Sprinkle rectangles with 1 cup pecans and cinnamon. Roll up jelly-roll style starting from a short side. Cut each log into 6 slices.

2. Generously grease 13×9-inch baking pan. Place rolls cut sides down in pan. Cover loosely with greased waxed paper and then with plastic wrap. Chill overnight. Cover and chill remaining **Eagle Brand**.

3. To bake, let pan of rolls stand at room temperature for 30 minutes. Preheat oven to 350°F. Bake 30 to 35 minutes or until golden brown. Cool in pan 5 minutes; loosen edges and remove rolls from pan.

4. Meanwhile for frosting, in small bowl, combine powdered sugar, remaining ⅓ cup **Eagle Brand** and vanilla. Drizzle frosting on warm rolls. Sprinkle with additional chopped pecans.   *Makes 12 rolls*

Creamy Cinnamon Roll

Hot Fudge Sauce

Prep Time: 10 minutes

1 (6-ounce) package semi-sweet chocolate chips (1 cup) *or*
   4 (1-ounce) squares semi-sweet chocolate
2 tablespoons butter or margarine
1 (14-ounce) can EAGLE® BRAND Sweetened Condensed
   Milk (NOT evaporated milk)
2 tablespoons water
1 teaspoon vanilla extract

1. In heavy saucepan, over medium heat, melt chips and butter with **Eagle Brand** and water. Cook and stir constantly until smooth. Stir in vanilla.

2. Serve warm over ice cream or as a fruit dipping sauce. Refrigerate leftovers.   *Makes 2 cups*

Microwave: In 1-quart glass measure, combine ingredients. Microwave at HIGH (100% power) 3 to 3½ minutes, stirring after each minute. Proceed as above.

To Reheat: In small heavy saucepan, combine desired amount of sauce with small amount of water. Over low heat, stir constantly until heated through.

Spirited Hot Fudge Sauce: Add ¼ cup almond, coffee, mint or orange-flavored liqueur with the vanilla.

Left to right: Hot Fudge Sauce,
Dulce de Leche (page 71)

DECADENT DELIGHTS

Quick Chocolate Mousse

Prep Time: 5 minutes

1 (14-ounce) can EAGLE® BRAND Sweetened Condensed
    Milk (NOT evaporated milk)
1 (4-serving size) package chocolate flavor instant pudding
    mix
1 cup cold water
1 cup (½ pint) whipping cream, whipped

1. In large mixing bowl, beat **Eagle Brand**, pudding mix and water;
chill 5 minutes.

2. Fold in whipped cream. Spoon into serving dishes; chill. Garnish as
desired.   *Makes 8 to 10 servings*

Creamy Mocha Latte

Prep Time: 5 minutes   Freeze Time: 2 hours

¾ cup water
2 tablespoons ground espresso
2 cups milk
1 (14-ounce) can EAGLE® BRAND Creamy Chocolate
    Sweetened Condensed Milk (NOT evaporated milk)
1 pint coffee ice cream, softened

1. Microwave ¾ cup water and ground espresso in 1-cup glass
measuring cup at HIGH (100% power) 1 minute.

2. Let stand 1 minute. Pour through a coffee filter, discarding grounds.

3. Stir together milk and coffee; pour into ice cube trays and freeze
2 hours. Process half the **Eagle Brand**, half of the ice cream and half
of coffee ice cubes in a blender until smooth, stopping to scrape down
sides.

4. Repeat procedure with remaining ingredients; serve immediately.
                                      Makes 6 cups

Creamy Hot Chocolate

Prep Time: 8 to 10 minutes

**1 (14-ounce) can EAGLE® BRAND Sweetened Condensed
    Milk (NOT evaporated milk)**
½ cup unsweetened cocoa powder
1½ teaspoons vanilla extract
⅛ teaspoon salt
6½ cups hot water
    Marshmallows (optional)

1. In large saucepan over medium heat, combine Eagle Brand, cocoa, vanilla and salt; mix well.

2. Slowly stir in water. Heat through, stirring occasionally. Do not boil. Top with marshmallows, if desired. Store covered in refrigerator.

Makes about 2 quarts

Microwave Directions: In 2-quart glass measure, combine all ingredients except marshmallows. Microwave at HIGH (100% power) 8 to 10 minutes, stirring every 3 minutes. Top with marshmallows, if desired. Store covered in refrigerator.

 *Helpful Hint*

Hot chocolate can be stored in the refrigerator for up to 5 days. Mix well and reheat before serving.

DECADENT DELIGHTS

Holiday Treasures

Easy Egg Nog Pound Cake

Prep Time: 10 minutes   Bake Time: 40 to 45 minutes

1 (18¼-ounce) package yellow cake mix
1 (4-serving size) package instant vanilla flavor pudding
   and pie filling mix
¾ cup BORDEN® Egg Nog
¾ cup vegetable oil
4 eggs
½ teaspoon ground nutmeg
   Powdered sugar (optional)

1. Preheat oven to 350°F.

2. In large mixing bowl, combine cake mix, pudding mix, **Borden Egg Nog** and oil; beat on low speed until moistened. Add eggs and nutmeg; beat on medium-high speed 4 minutes.

3. Pour into greased and floured 10-inch fluted or tube pan.

4. Bake 40 to 45 minutes or until toothpick inserted near center comes out clean.

5. Cool 10 minutes; remove from pan. Cool completely. Sprinkle with powdered sugar, if desired.   *Makes 1 (10-inch) cake*

Holiday Egg Nog Punch

Prep Time: 5 minutes

2 (1-quart) cans BORDEN® Egg Nog, chilled
1 (12-ounce) can frozen orange juice concentrate, thawed
1 cup cold water
Orange sherbet

1. In large pitcher combine all ingredients except sherbet; mix well.

2. Just before serving, pour into punch bowl; top with scoops of sherbet. Refrigerate leftovers.   *Makes about 1 quart*

Cherry-Berry Crumble

Prep Time: 10 minutes

1 (21-ounce) can cherry pie filling
2 cups fresh or frozen raspberries
1 (14-ounce) can EAGLE® BRAND Sweetened Condensed
     Milk (NOT evaporated milk)
1½ cups granola

1. In medium-sized saucepan, cook and stir cherry pie filling and raspberries until heated through. Stir in **Eagle Brand**; cook and stir 1 minute more.

2. Spoon into 2-quart square baking dish or 6 individual dessert dishes. Sprinkle with granola. Serve warm.   *Makes 6 servings*

Peach-Berry Crumble: Substitute peach pie filling for cherry pie filling.

Cherry-Rhubarb Crumble: Substitute fresh or frozen sliced rhubarb for the raspberries. In medium-sized saucepan, cook and stir pie filling and rhubarb until bubbly. Cook and stir 5 minutes more. Proceed as directed above.

Apple Mince Pie

Prep Time: 30 minutes   Bake Time: 35 minutes

Pastry for 2-crust pie
1 (27-ounce) jar NONE SUCH® Ready-to-Use Mincemeat
    (Regular or Brandy & Rum)
3 medium all-purpose apples, cored, peeled and thinly
    sliced
3 tablespoons flour
2 tablespoons butter or margarine, melted
1 egg yolk *plus* **2 tablespoons water, mixed**

1. Place rack in lower half of oven; preheat oven to 425°F. Turn mincemeat into pastry-lined 9-inch pie plate.

2. In large bowl, toss apples with flour and butter; spoon evenly over mincemeat. Cover with top crust; cut slits near center. Seal and flute. Brush egg mixture over crust.

3. Bake 10 minutes. *Reduce oven temperature to 375°F;* bake 25 minutes longer or until golden. Cool. Garnish as desired.

Makes 1 (9-inch) pie

 *Helpful Hint*

1 (9-ounce) package **None Such®** *Condensed Mincemeat, reconstituted as package directs, can be substituted for* **None Such®** *Ready-to-Use Mincemeat.*

Versatile Cut-Out Cookies

Prep Time: 15 minutes   Bake Time: 7 to 9 minutes

3⅓ cups all-purpose flour
1 tablespoon baking powder
½ teaspoon salt
1 (14-ounce) can EAGLE® BRAND Sweetened Condensed Milk (NOT evaporated milk)
¾ cup (1½ sticks) butter or margarine, softened
2 eggs
2 teaspoons vanilla extract *or* 1½ teaspoons almond or lemon extract
Ready-to-spread frosting

1. Preheat oven to 350°F. Grease baking sheets; set aside. In medium bowl, combine flour, baking powder and salt; set aside. In large bowl, beat **Eagle Brand,** butter, eggs and vanilla until well blended. Add dry ingredients; mix well.

2. On floured surface, lightly knead dough to form smooth ball. Divide into thirds. On well-floured surface, roll out each portion to ⅛-inch thickness. Cut with floured cookie cutter. Place 1 inch apart on prepared sheets.

3. Bake 7 to 9 minutes or until lightly browned around edges. Cool completely. Frost and decorate as desired. Store loosely covered at room temperature.   *Makes about 6½ dozen cookies*

Sandwich Cookies: Use 2½-inch cookie cutter. Bake as directed above. Sandwich two cookies together with ready-to-spread frosting. Sprinkle with powdered sugar or colored sugar, if desired. Makes about 3 dozen cookies.

Versatile Cut-Out Cookies

Chocolate Snowswirl Fudge

Prep Time: 10 minutes   Chill Time: 2 hours

3 cups (18 ounces) semi-sweet chocolate chips
1 (14-ounce) can EAGLE® BRAND Sweetened Condensed
 Milk (NOT evaporated milk)
4 tablespoons butter or margarine, divided
1½ teaspoons vanilla extract
 Dash salt
1 cup chopped nuts
2 cups miniature marshmallows

1. Melt chips with **Eagle Brand**, 2 tablespoons butter, vanilla and salt. Remove from heat; stir in nuts. Spread evenly into foil-lined 8- or 9-inch square pan.

2. Melt marshmallows with remaining 2 tablespoons butter. Spread on top of fudge. With table knife or metal spatula, swirl through top of fudge.

3. Chill at least 2 hours or until firm. Turn fudge onto cutting board; peel off foil and cut into squares. Store loosely covered at room temperature.   *Makes about 2 pounds*

 *Helpful Hint*

Serve this decorative fudge in individual gold and silver paper candy cups or give as a gift in a small silver tin decorated with white ribbons.

Traditional Pumpkin Pie

Prep Time: 20 minutes   Bake Time: 50 to 55 minutes

1 (15-ounce) can pumpkin
1 (14-ounce) can EAGLE® BRAND Sweetened Condensed
**   Milk (NOT evaporated milk)**
2 eggs
1 teaspoon ground cinnamon
½ teaspoon ground ginger
½ teaspoon ground nutmeg
½ teaspoon salt
1 (9-inch) unbaked pastry shell
Topping (recipes follow, optional)

1. Preheat oven to 425°F. In large mixing bowl, combine all ingredients except pastry shell and Topping; mix well.

2. Pour into prepared pastry shell. Bake 15 minutes.

3. *Reduce oven temperature to 350°F.* Continue baking 35 to 40 minutes, or as directed with one of the Toppings, or until knife inserted 1 inch from edge comes out clean. Cool. Garnish as desired. Store covered in refrigerator.   *Makes 1 (9-inch) pie*

Sour Cream Topping: In medium bowl, combine 1½ cups sour cream, 2 tablespoons sugar and 1 teaspoon vanilla extract. After pie has baked 30 minutes at 350°F, spread evenly over top; bake 10 minutes.

Streusel Topping: In medium bowl, combine ½ cup packed brown sugar and ½ cup all-purpose flour; cut in ¼ cup (½ stick) cold butter or margarine until crumbly. Stir in ¼ cup chopped nuts. After pie has baked 30 minutes at 350°F, sprinkle evenly over top; bake 10 minutes.

Chocolate Glaze: In small saucepan over low heat, melt ½ cup semi-sweet chocolate chips and 1 teaspoon solid shortening. Drizzle or spread over top of baked and cooled pie.

Maple Pumpkin Cheesecake

Prep Time: 25 minutes   Bake Time: 1 hour and 15 minutes
Cool Time: 1 hour   Chill Time: 4 hours

1¼ **cups graham cracker crumbs**
¼ **cup sugar**
¼ **cup (½ stick) butter or margarine, melted**
3 **(8-ounce) packages cream cheese, softened**
1 **(14-ounce) can EAGLE® BRAND Sweetened Condensed Milk (NOT evaporated milk)**
1 **(15-ounce) can pumpkin**
3 **eggs**
¼ **cup maple syrup**
1½ **teaspoons ground cinnamon**
1 **teaspoon ground nutmeg**
½ **teaspoon salt**
   Maple Pecan Glaze (recipe follows)

1. Preheat oven to 325°F. Combine graham cracker crumbs, sugar and butter; press firmly on bottom of 9-inch springform pan.* With mixer, beat cream cheese until fluffy. Gradually beat in **Eagle Brand** until smooth. Add pumpkin, eggs, maple syrup, cinnamon, nutmeg and salt; mix well. Pour into prepared pan. Bake 1¼ hours or until center appears nearly set when shaken. Cool 1 hour. Cover and chill at least 4 hours.

2. To serve, spoon some Maple Pecan Sauce over cheesecake. Garnish with whipped cream and pecans if desired. Pass remaining sauce. Store leftovers covered in refrigerator.

Makes 1 (9-inch) cheesecake

To use 13×9-inch baking pan, press crumb mixture firmly on bottom of pan. Proceed as directed above, except bake 50 to 60 minutes or until center appears nearly set when shaken.

Maple Pecan Glaze: In saucepan, combine ¾ cup maple syrup and 1 cup (½ pint) whipping cream; bring to a boil. Boil rapidly 15 to 20 minutes or until thickened; stir occasionally. Add ½ cup chopped pecans.

Maple Pumpkin Cheesecake

Chocolate Cranberry Bars

Prep Time: 15 minutes   Bake Time: 25 to 30 minutes

2 cups vanilla wafer crumbs
½ cup unsweetened cocoa powder
3 tablespoons sugar
⅔ cup (1⅓ sticks) cold butter, cut into pieces
1 (14-ounce) can EAGLE® BRAND Sweetened Condensed Milk (NOT evaporated milk)
1 cup peanut butter-flavored chips
1⅓ cups (6-ounce package) sweetened dried cranberries or raisins
1 cup finely chopped walnuts

1. Heat oven to 350°F. Stir together wafer crumbs, cocoa and sugar in medium bowl; cut in butter until crumbly.

2. Press mixture evenly on bottom and ½ inch up sides of ungreased 13×9-inch baking pan. Pour **Eagle Brand** evenly over crumb mixture; sprinkle evenly on top with peanut butter chips, dried cranberries and nuts; press down firmly.

3. Bake 25 to 30 minutes or until lightly browned. Cool completely in pan on wire rack. Cover with foil; let stand several hours. Cut into bars. Store covered at room temperature.   *Make about 36 bars*

Peppermint Patties

Prep Time: 20 minutes

1 (14-ounce) can EAGLE® BRAND Sweetened Condensed
   Milk (NOT evaporated milk)
1 tablespoon peppermint extract
   Green or red food coloring (optional)
6 cups powdered sugar
   Additional powdered sugar
1½ pounds chocolate-flavored candy coating*, melted

*Also called confectionery coating or almond bark.

1. In large mixing bowl, combine **Eagle Brand**, extract and food coloring, if desired. Add 6 cups sugar; beat on low speed until smooth and well blended. Turn mixture onto surface sprinkled with additional powdered sugar.

2. Knead lightly to form smooth ball. Shape into 1-inch balls. Place 2 inches apart on waxed paper-lined baking sheets. Flatten each ball into a 1½-inch patty.

3. Let dry 1 hour or longer; turn over and let dry at least 1 hour. With fork, dip each patty into warm candy coating (draw fork lightly across rim of pan to remove excess coating). Invert onto waxed-paper-lined baking sheets; let stand until firm. Store covered at room temperature or in refrigerator.   *Makes about 8 dozen patties*

Holiday Cheese Tarts

Prep Time: 10 minutes   Chill Time: 2 hours

1 (8-ounce) package cream cheese, softened
1 (14-ounce) can EAGLE® BRAND Sweetened Condensed Milk (NOT evaporated milk)
⅓ cup REALEMON® Lemon Juice from Concentrate
1 teaspoon vanilla extract
2 (4-ounce) packages single serve graham cracker crumb pie crusts
Assorted fruit (strawberries, blueberries, bananas, raspberries, orange segments, cherries, kiwi fruit, grapes, pineapple, etc.)
¼ cup apple jelly, melted (optional)

1. With mixer, beat cream cheese until fluffy. Gradually beat in **Eagle Brand** until smooth. Stir in **ReaLemon** and vanilla.

2. Spoon into crusts. Chill 2 hours or until set. Just before serving, top with fruit; brush with jelly, if desired. Refrigerate leftovers.

Make 12 tarts

 *Helpful Hint*

To assure the very best results from your desserts, always use **Eagle® Brand** Sweetened Condensed Milk in recipes provided by Eagle Brand and follow the recipe exactly. Other sweetened condensed milk products may not be of the same high quality and may negatively affect Eagle Brand recipe performance.

Holiday Cheese Tarts

Holiday Pumpkin Treats

Prep Time: 25 minutes   Bake Time: 55 minutes

1¾ cups all-purpose flour
⅓ cup firmly packed brown sugar
⅓ cup granulated sugar
1 cup (2 sticks) cold butter or margarine
1 cup finely chopped nuts
1 (27-ounce) jar **NONE SUCH®** Ready-to-Use Mincemeat (Regular or Brandy & Rum)
1 (15-ounce) can pumpkin
1 (14-ounce) can **EAGLE® BRAND** Sweetened Condensed Milk (NOT evaporated milk)
2 eggs
1 teaspoon ground cinnamon
½ teaspoon ground allspice
½ teaspoon salt

1. Preheat oven to 425°F. Combine flour and sugars; cut in butter until crumbly. Stir in nuts. Reserve 1½ cups crumb mixture; press remaining crumb mixture on bottom and halfway up sides of 13×9-inch baking pan. Spoon **None Such** over crust.

2. Combine remaining ingredients except reserved crumb mixture; mix well. Pour over **None Such**. Top with reserved crumb mixture.

3. Bake 15 minutes. *Reduce oven temperature to 350°F.* Bake 40 minutes longer or until golden brown around edges. Cool. Cut into squares. Serve warm or at room temperature. Refrigerate leftovers.

Makes 36 bars

 *Helpful Hint*

You can top this dessert with scoops of ice cream prior to serving, if desired.

INDEX

METRIC CONVERSION CHART

VOLUME MEASUREMENTS (dry)

1/8 teaspoon = 0.5 mL
1/4 teaspoon = 1 mL
1/2 teaspoon = 2 mL
3/4 teaspoon = 4 mL
1 teaspoon = 5 mL
1 tablespoon = 15 mL
2 tablespoons = 30 mL
1/4 cup = 60 mL
1/3 cup = 75 mL
1/2 cup = 125 mL
2/3 cup = 150 mL
3/4 cup = 175 mL
1 cup = 250 mL
2 cups = 1 pint = 500 mL
3 cups = 750 mL
4 cups = 1 quart = 1 L

VOLUME MEASUREMENTS (fluid)

1 fluid ounce (2 tablespoons) = 30 mL
4 fluid ounces (1/2 cup) = 125 mL
8 fluid ounces (1 cup) = 250 mL
12 fluid ounces (1 1/2 cups) = 375 mL
16 fluid ounces (2 cups) = 500 mL

WEIGHTS (mass)

1/2 ounce = 15 g
1 ounce = 30 g
3 ounces = 90 g
4 ounces = 120 g
8 ounces = 225 g
10 ounces = 285 g
12 ounces = 360 g
16 ounces = 1 pound = 450 g

DIMENSIONS

1/16 inch = 2 mm
1/8 inch = 3 mm
1/4 inch = 6 mm
1/2 inch = 1.5 cm
3/4 inch = 2 cm
1 inch = 2.5 cm

OVEN TEMPERATURES

250°F = 120°C
275°F = 140°C
300°F = 150°C
325°F = 160°C
350°F = 180°C
375°F = 190°C
400°F = 200°C
425°F = 220°C
450°F = 230°C

BAKING PAN SIZES

Utensil	Size in Inches/Quarts	Metric Volume	Size in Centimeters
Baking or Cake Pan (square or rectangular)	8×8×2	2 L	20×20×5
	9×9×2	2.5 L	23×23×5
	12×8×2	3 L	30×20×5
	13×9×2	3.5 L	33×23×5
Loaf Pan	8×4×3	1.5 L	20×10×7
	9×5×3	2 L	23×13×7
Round Layer Cake Pan	8×1½	1.2 L	20×4
	9×1½	1.5 L	23×4
Pie Plate	8×1¼	750 mL	20×3
	9×1¼	1 L	23×3
Baking Dish or Casserole	1 quart	1 L	—
	1½ quart	1.5 L	—
	2 quart	2 L	—